Syllables Of Eternity

For the love, the god, and the grief that didn't answer

Vaishnavi Alur

BookLeaf Publishing

India | USA | UK

Made with ❤ on the BookLeaf Publishing Platform
www.bookleafpub.in
www.bookleafpub.com

Dedication

For the ones who stayed, and the ones who didn't.
To the ghosts who never learned how to haunt me right.
And to the ones who saw me, whole and undone,
who stayed even when I made leaving easy.

This is for you.
You know who you are.

Preface

This is not a book of poems.
It is a collection of aftermaths.

""Syllables of Eternity" - was never meant to be written.It
simply became-like grief. Like love. Like all the things
we never truly choose, but live through anyway.

I wrote when love was too big for the body.When death
didn't come with answers.When all I had was the echo of
being alive and not knowing why.This book was not written
to impress.It was written because I could not carry it alone
anymore.
There is no performance in these pages, no obligation to
resolve or inspire-
only the honesty that spilled out when I stopped trying to be
understood.Only the tenderness that survived, despite being
told it was weakness.

This is not a curated collection. It is a raw archive-
a record of moments I didn't think anyone else felt, but wrote
down anyway, just in case.

But if you are here, reading this, then maybe something in

these pages already knows you.Maybe something in them
stayed behind just to keep you company.If you are here,
reading this, then something in you is still searching.

And if a single line unsettles you, if it makes you remember
what you buried so well-
then this book has done what it came here to do. If these
poems ache, let them.If they don't make sense, that's fine.
They weren't made to.They weren't made for
admiration.They were made for witnessing.

These are the syllables I could no longer swallow.
These are my syllables of eternity.

— *Vaishnavi Alur*

Acknowledgements

To my cat-thank you for letting me just be-
 for letting me simply exist beside you, without having to
explain myself.

To my Mimmi, Dad, and Anna-
you didn't get a say in loving me, you were bound to love me
by blood, but thank you for choosing, every single day.
Even when I was difficult to understand. Even when I wasn't
easy to root for.

To my Doby-
you didn't ask to be the reason behind most of these pages,
but here we are. Thank you for becoming the reason I put
words to what I had buried.

To Sanjay Sir, Jaishree Ma'am and Subreen Ma'am - thank you
for proving that guidance isn't about rules, but about seeing
someone when they forget they exist. To Parth, thank you for
proving that family doesn't always come through blood. To
my friends- thank you for leaving and staying. For all the
lessons - even if it's showing what real friendship means, and

even if it cost us. And to the people I've outgrown-thank you for showing me that I could.

And to my younger self- thank you for never erasing us. I won't let all of that be for nothing. We're not done, and this achievement and story is finally ours.

1. To love is to witness,

The truth is simple-
the closer you crawl beneath someone's skin,
the more their cracks run deep,
like fault lines waiting to split.
This is how marriages burn to ash,
how children grow wings to escape,
how friendship, once solid,
crumbles like paper beneath water.

You think you know love-
until you've watched someone unravel,
frayed and threadbare.
Until you've seen them starving, teeth clenched in
silence,
or held their shaking hand
while their world fell apart in pieces.

Love is not soft;
it is the muscle that aches, the bone that breaks,
the decision to bear the weight of another's wreckage,
to cradle their filthy heart,
and whisper, stay.
Love is a fistfight with yourself,
the quiet surrender to a battlefield that never clears.

It's standing in the eye of the storm
when every instinct tells you to run.

I adore the wreckage, the unwashed sheets,
the rooms littered with empty bottles and sleepless
nights.
I adore the moment when
people drink too much and crumble,
when they stand at the edge of themselves,
raw and tender as new skin.
I adore the slip of realization in their eyes
when love blooms like a bruise,
unexpected and cruel.

The way they wake, startled,
gasping in the haze of the morning,
the world foreign around them.
I love the sound when a heart breaks,
the breath stolen when their favorite character dies-
a grief so pure it makes them more alive than they've
ever been.

I fall in love with people's undoing,
with their mascara-smeared faces,
their hands trembling in forgotten prayers.
I fall in love with their daydreams,
their eyes lost in a world just out of reach,

with their silence, with their storms, with their
surrender.

There is nothing more holy than when they fall apart.
Nothing more beautiful than truth too brutal to bear.
Show me your ruin-
and I will call it love.

\

2. I never prayed for this,

I never looked up at the stars or prayed for Cupid to bring us together.
This love isn't a gift from the divine, nor some twist of fate.
I twisted the threads of destiny with my own hands,
pulling them tight until they bled his name.

This love is not some accident it's the knowing that-
I'd trade anything any piece of myself-
to be the one who makes him smile,
to hold that fragile joy in my hands,
to keep it safe even if everything else around me falls apart.

All I want is to hold his laughter close,
to tuck it away in the quiet places of my mind,
to carry it with me through the long, lonely nights.
Isn't that enough to make all the hurt worth it?

How could I not love him,
when he took a world that felt empty
and painted it with colors I thought had faded forever?
How could I not love him,

when he filled every quiet space that I had learned to live with,
when he brought a warmth I never thought I'd feel again?

In my dreams, I find my way back to him,
and for a brief, sacred moment,
every wound, every scar,
every heartache I've carried-
suddenly feels like it all led to this-to him.

Maybe to him,
this is all just a passing thing a season that changes,
a breath in the cold.
But I would rewrite the constellations in the sky-
if it meant to keep his light from ever going out of my life.

3. Anatomy of Shrinking

I was thirteen when I first learned that home is not
where you live,
but where your absence does not go unnoticed.
I told my mother, "I do not belong anywhere," and
she told me I should not feel that way.
As if belonging was a choice,
as if I had not spent years splitting myself into
shapes small enough to fit into their expectations.

I taught myself how to shrink-
How to trade hunger for numbers,
sleep for a brighter report card,
my voice for a silence they could be proud of.
And still,
it was never enough.

I stitched myself into their version of me,
but the seams just kept unraveling.
I have done everything with these hands-
bled for love that only held me by the throat,
rewrote myself in ink and bone
to fit the space they allowed me.

I have torn myself apart just to be small enough,

quiet enough, enough.
I mistook love for anything that stayed
Even when it hollowed me out,
even when it made a home of my ruin.

I let hands hold me like a lesson,
like something to be taught obedience.
And when they called me too much,
I learned how to be less.
When they called me ungrateful,
I swallowed my ache like it was shameful to have.

They tell me what I should be,
a daughter first, a name second,
a shadow of their expectations-
stitched into my skin.
I speak and it is a crime.
I love and it is a betrayal.
I exist and it is an inconvenience.

They say a house on fire still casts warmth,
but I have only ever felt the burning.
And yet,
I am the one being blamed for the smoke.

I was thirteen when I learned-
that home was not a place,

but a debt to be repaid.

That love was conditional,
measured in grades and obedience,
that my body was not my own but
-a vessel,
to carry their pride and never my own.

I have burned myself down -
to be what they wanted,
held my tongue till it rotted in my mouth,
handed over my voice and called it devotion.

And still-
still, I am never enough.

I reach for something-
a hand, a place, a whisper that says
I belong-
but the walls close in, the world shrinks,
and I am left standing in the wreckage of someone -
I was never allowed to be.

4. Where the void ends,

I have walked through deserts of people,
parched by conversations that never touched me,
brushed by hands that only skimmed the surface.
And when I thought I was drowning in this void,
he wrapped me in himself.
And suddenly, I could breathe.

If I could choose where to fall,
it would be there.
Not ground. Not void.
But in the arms that feel like life itself.

Because I have walked through this world starving,
but his touch fed me.
I have lived like a ghost,
but his warmth made me real.
Do you know what it is to find everything
in something as simple as touch?

His arms? Home.
Not a place sought,
but the one that erased the need for seeking.

Give me his storms,

and I will bare my chest to lightning.
I would rip apart my soul
to piece together his peace.

Tear down heaven, brick by brick,
if it meant the sky never fell on him.
His pain-
mine to swallow.
His battles-
mine to lose.
And if fate were to take it all,
it wouldn't matter.
To die in those arms
would still feel like living.

What I wanted, what I craved,
was already given to me
the moment his arms tightened
around the pieces of me
I thought no one could hold.

Ache, oh ache-
not the kind that breaks you,
but the kind that reminds you:
You are alive.

Yet within his arms,

even the sharpest edges of my fears dulled.
Even the shadows I had fed for years-
lost their teeth.

Cut me open.
Carve his sufferings into my ribs,
and I would bear it with reverence.

But what broke me most?

I'd never ask for anything in return.
His peace was enough.
His breath against my neck,
the weight of his silence-
prayers answered.

And maybe that's what love is.

Not the need to be held,
but the willingness to bear-
to carry without question,
to suffer without demand.

I never needed more than what he gave me.
But still, he gave.

His arms did not just hold me.

They swallowed me whole.
Not in the way night consumes the sky,
but like the earth cradles a seed-
delicate and steady,
until it is ready to grow.

Every broken part of me found its place there.
Not fixed. Not healed.
Accepted.

As if my cracks were what made me beautiful.
To die there,
pressed against the ache of his existence,
would not be an end.

It would be the deepest form of being alive.

Because in his arms,
I found every reason to live.
Every reason to burn, to shatter,
to feel every inch of my soul unravel.

5. Language of your ruin,

If you'd let me,
I'd plunge into the chasm of you,
* where the darkness sits,*
and unravel the knots,
you've tied around your soul.

I'd find your cracks,
trace them with trembling hands,
and weave them into something sacred-
a tapestry of fragmentation,
that only I would dare to cherish.

You don't understand,
how your torment is the prayer I utter,
how the stillness of your heart is the only rhythm I
know.

I'd crawl into your abyss,
build a home from the shards you hide,
cradle the fractured remnants of your being,

and show you -

how even your emptiness,

can become a language
I've learned to speak-
and tell you, with a truth so heavy,
that even in your destruction,
you are the only salvation I'll ever seek.

6. Proof of the blade

I pull the blade from my own ribs,
wipe it clean, hand it over-
but somehow, it still ends up in my back.
I say sorry before I bleed,
before I even know if I've done the cutting.
Before their silence carves into me.
They say I do not listen.
That my love lands like shrapnel,
splitting skin where it was meant to mend.
I never mean to wound-
but what does meaning matter
when the blood is real?
I stand trial in their eyes,
no gavel, no verdict-just the knowing.
That I was never enough to begin with.
That I must have been the wound-
before I even opened my mouth.

Maybe I was always meant to be collateral damage,
a lesson in love measured by absence.
A mirror that only reflects
what people never wanted to see in themselves.

They say I wound them, and I believe it-

not because I taste the blade in my throat,
but because their voices make it true.

I have never asked for mercy.
I have never begged to be the one spared.
Only-
how many times can a knife call itself the hand?

How many times can a body bear
the weight of its own undoing before it simply-
stays undone?
How many times do you let a house burn before you
admit that the match is in your own hands?
That maybe the smoke is not a warning, but a requiem-
for the version of me that was almost enough.

I have spent a lifetime picking glass from my throat,
swallowing down the urge to say-
I do not want to be this.

I fold my words into the smallest spaces,
press them so deep they become marrow,
and still,
they slip through my teeth like sins I didn't mean to
commit.

But silence does not absolve, only festers.

And when I finally speak,
it is always too little, too late.

Maybe this is justice,
to be made the villain in the stories
I was only trying to survive.

7. Spine of fire, hands of ash

I would kneel,
not in reverence, but in surrender-
bare hands pressed to the earth,
bones unclasped,
offering every inch of me like an open wound.

Let them call it weakness,
let them call it madness
I will still crawl to you.
I would strip my name from my throat,
let it unspool like thread between your fingers.

Let them say I am reckless, unmoored,
lost-as if I care for dignity,
as if I care for pride-
I care only for you.

I would let the world spit its warnings into my ear,
let it whisper of ruin, of shame, of consequence.

Let them say I am nothing
but a girl unspined,
a body bent into worship.
Let them say I am burning

as if I would not burn for you.

I would tear myself at the seams,
pull apart the fabric of who I was meant to be,
leave every expectation bleeding at your feet.

They ask me what love is.
I tell them: this-

A quiet undoing. A reckoning.
A fire I would walk into, hands open,
again and again and again.

8. Breath, Tangled.

I have heard that time is counted in accomplishments,
in the weight of what we -
build, break, and barter away.
That a day must be filled with movement,
that stillness is waste,
that love must prove itself in labor.

But if I wake at 6:58 AM
and your breath is tangled in mine,
if my hands memorize the map of your spine,
if I spend a minute-
just one-
learning how your heartbeat speaks in syllables
I am still learning to pronounce,
then I have done more than all the clocks
ticking their accusations against the walls.

Because the world asks for monuments,
for things it can touch and take,
for proof that love is worth the time it steals.

But I have found that devotion is-
not measured in miles walked away,
but in the softness of staying.

And if the only thing I build today -
is the courage to hold you when the world is unkind
then let history call me useless.

I will have lived enough to be remembered.

9. Something hurts, Ellis.

The heart stops-not the way it should,
not like a quiet slipping, a gentle fading,
but like a train derailing at full speed,
like metal screeching against itself,
trying to hold on to motion that isn't there.
It doesn't die. It lingers.

A pulse that stutters,
as if it has no business being alive.
Air lodges somewhere between my throat and lungs-
not quite breath, not quite silence.
It clogs, thick and unmoving, choking the voice
I don't have the strength to find.

Inhale-
it burns like surrender.
Exhale-
it tastes like every lie I've swallowed whole.

I am heavy.
Heavier than the world allows me to be.
A rock in the chest that won't sink,
because it isn't the weight-it's the ocean itself,
pulling, pulling, pulling, but never letting go.

My eyes-
once brimming with oceans now,
hold nothing but rain that never had the courage to fall.
They don't blink; they pour.
Not in relief, not in release,
but in the way a dam breaks-
all at once, all too much, drowning everything in its
path.

I bite my lips,
taste iron-the sharp tang of something alive,
something that wants to stay,
something that doesn't belong to me.
It tastes like failure,
like being too much but never enough.

The cuts-
thin at first, then deep.
We've been here before.
They are the ghosts I carry, the proof I exist.
They whisper that pain is the only thing that stays,
the only thing that will ever remember my name.

Something hurts, Ellis.
But it's not a wound you can stitch,
not a bruise you can ice.

It's a crack in the bones,
a splintering where nothing should ever grow.

And then comes the numbness.
Like an old friend who never knocks,
burn line beneat yeashing
untill even the hurt forgets the shape of its own body.

And I sink
Not in defeat,
but in the way the ocean sinks into itself-
unapologetically, completely,
letting the weight of it all pull me home.

10. When the world blinks,

Did it happen all at once?
Did the world just blink one second here, the next gone?
Or did it stretch, slow and merciless,
like a string pulled too thin before it snaps?

Did it whisper first?
Did you feel it curling in the corners of your body,
pressing behind your ribs,
tapping at your pulse like a secret trying to be told?

Did you fight it?
Did your hands reach for something anything or did
they just fall,
useless, like a bird that forgot how to fly?

Did you think of me?
Did my name flicker, even for a second?
Did you remember the time l asked if people know when
they are about to die?
And if you did, did you want to say, yes?

Was it lonely?
Or was something there, something waiting not cold, not
cruel, but quiet,

like a mother shushing the world to sleep?

I don't mean to ask too much.
Just-
I just need to know.
Did it hurt?
Or did it finally stop?

11. I burn, therefore I am.

This pain of mine has a purpose to serve.
I do not waver. I do not kneel.

I have been both the blade and the wound,
the storm and the wreckage,
the sinner and the sacrifice.
I have watched my own hands ruin me.
shredded myself down to please a world-
that never once learned how to hold me right.

I have carved myself into shapes
for visitors who never stayed.
bled out pieces of me for hands that never reached back-
and still, I was the one left to sweep away the remains.
But no more.

I will not betray the child
who once stood in front of mirrors,
her eyes full of dreams too big for her body.

Whispering-
to the stars as if they could hear her.
Believing-
that even in the darkness, that she was meant for more.

I will not kneel before the weight of my past,
nor break beneath the sins the world cast upon me.

Let God count them all
He will find their hands in my ruin.
And if his judgement must come, let it.
I will face Him and walk backward into hell
before I bow to anything less than the fire inside me.

Because I have been to hell already.
I have built a home there.
lit the candles with the ashes of my own forgieness.
furnished it with every moment I swallowed my
screams.

And still, I rise.
Still, I stand.
For her.

For the girl who was stranded and alone.
For the child who dreamed,
who once whispered -
don't forget me.
For the woman who will make sure
she never feels that way again.

I will not fall. Not now. Not ever.
This pain of mine has a purpose to serve.

And if it must burn,
then let it burn bright enough
to set the whole damn sky on fire.
No grave will hold me.
no fire will burn me, no past will chain me.
I will walk forward.

For her.
For the child who dared to dream.

And no god, no force,
no hand in this world
will make me kneel again.

12. Unseen, Unforgotten.

I used to treat your presence like a closed door-
eyes fixed forward, hands steady,
pretending the key never burned in my palm.

But now-
my gaze is a traitor.
It finds you before I do,
before I even think to stop it,
like a needle drawn to a wound it knows too well.

And the moment it happens,
the second our eyes meet,
I tear away like a coward.
Like someone afraid of how quickly
a glance can become a reckoning.

I wonder if you feel it too-
the way the air knots itself between us,
how the silence-
between two heartbeats is the loudest sound in the room.

When you stand too close,
I forget the shape of my own body.
The breath in my throat turns to static,

the space between us feels like a question
neither of us is willing to answer.

Do you look for me too?
Or am I just another ghost in your periphery-
here, gone, forgotten?

But even if I am, I won't let it fade.
I'll carve this feeling into permanence,
let it live beneath my skin like something holy,
like something ruinous.

Because even if you never see me-
I will never let you be unseen.

13. How could I not?

I wish my eyes could write you the way they see you-
how light clings to your face like it's trying to stay,
how your hands carry the weight of the world
but never reach for anything yourself.

You pour love like a downpour,
but never let yourself stand in the rain.
You see beauty in everything-
except the body that houses your own heart.

I wish you could hear yourself the way I do-
your voice, not just sound, but a pulse,
your laugh, not just noise, but a reason.
And if I could bottle it,
I'd smash the glass with my bare hands-
just to hear it again.

14. Eleven

I tell myself I have moved on,
that time has scrubbed you from my bones,
that my hands no longer shape themselves around your
absence.

But then someone says, It's 11:11,
and I am back where I swore I'd never be-
palms empty, breath caught,
body waiting for a miracle I do not believe in.

I do not wish for you.
Not anymore. Not in the way I used to.
Not with the kind of hope that turns hunger into
worship.

But some wounds do not close,
they only learn how to ache quietly.
And maybe that is all I have ever been-
a collection of almost-healed scars,
a body that flinches before the knife even falls.

It is 11:11.
I do not make a wish.

But I still pause-
as if grief, like love, might still be listening.

34

15. Not in this life, not in the next.

I will know you.
Even if the world rips itself apart and
rebuilds a thousand times over,
even if we are nothing but echoes in someone else's
dream-
I will find you.

Maybe not in ways that make sense-
Maybe you will not be flesh,
but something softer,
something I maybe cannot name.
Maybe you will be the weight
 in my chest when the night is too quiet,
or the way my hands still reach for something missing.

Maybe I will love you in ways that don't need names.
As the stranger whose laugh stops me in my tracks.
As the book I pull from a shelf without knowing why.
As the song I hum before I ever learn the words.

Maybe I will never know you at all.
Maybe I will spend a lifetime chasing ghosts.
Maybe I will wake up one morning,

feel the sun on my skin,
and ache for something I cannot touch.

But if I do find you-
if you stand before me,
with eyes I should not remember but do,
with a voice that feels like home in a place I've never
been-

Know this:
I will not let you go.
Not in this life, not in the next, not in the thousand after
that.

16. Mouthful of Petals

I don't know what part of me is still breaking,
only that it never stops-
That I keep moving like a body bracing for impact,
like I am always waiting for the next hit.

I wake up tired.
Not the kind sleep can fix-
the kind that sits in the bones,
that drags in my chest like I have swallowed the weight
of myself.

There are days I swear I am fine,
that I laugh at the right moments,
that I nod in the right places,
that I make eye contact without my hands shaking-
but then I am alone,
and my reflection is staring back like it knows I am
lying.

I keep saying it will pass.
Like grief is a train that knows when to stop,
like sorrow follows the rules of departure,
like pain ever really leaves-
but I know better.

Some wounds don't heal.
They settle.
They dig their roots in the quiet of your ribs,
build temples in the bruises,
and wait-
not to hurt,
just to remind you that you survived something you still
don't have words for.

17. They tried to take away this too.

They never warn you what happens
when you love something too much.

The world does not stand by-
it tightens its grip,
pries it from your hands like a thief
who watches you cradle it,
waits for the moment your heart swells too full
before it rips it away.

I have seen this before.
Love torn from fingers curled too tightly around it,
smiles fading mid-laughter,
people walking away with pieces they never give back.

And now it is my turn, isn't it?
To watch as they carve him out of my life
with dull, rusted knives,
slow and deliberate-
not with force, but with reasons.
With silence. With rules wrapped in care.

I do not beg.

I do not waver.
I do not crumble beneath their careful destruction.

I stand, spine straight, jaw locked,
as they explain why I should be patient,
why I should let go,
why I should trust that the world knows better
than my own heart.

"Be wise. Be grateful. Step back."

As if love is something to be measured,
as if distance is anything but starvation.
As if their hands are not the ones holding the blade
pressing against my ribs,
waiting for me to make it easy,
waiting for me to hand over the only thing
that has ever felt like home.

But love does not fold in on itself.
It does not learn obedience.
It does not bow just because they say it should.

Let them turn away,
let them strip me down to bone and breath-
I will still hold this fire in my chest.

Because love does not die in silence.
It does not shrink just because it is told to.
It lingers in the spaces they cannot touch,
thrives in the cracks they cannot seal.

They can take him from my hands,
but they will never take him from my story.
And that is where love lives.

Unmoved. Unfinished.
Mine.

18. If nothing else,

I will never be a poem-
not the kind that lingers on tongues,
not the kind people recite under their breath like
scripture.

No one will press their lips to my name.
No one will hold me between their hands
like something sacred.

I will never be a song-
not the kind that sneaks into memories,
not the kind you catch yourself humming at red lights.
I will not be played twice.
I will not be remembered in the quiet of a night drive.

I will never be a story-
not the kind that keeps you up past midnight,
not the kind that makes you forget the world outside its
pages.

I am the chapter you skipped.
The ending you never turned back for.
The sentence you almost highlighted-
but didn't.

But if nothing else, I will be yours.

Not in the way ink clings to paper,
not in the way a melody lingers in the throat,
not in the way a story is passed down-
but in the way a room still holds the scent of someone
long after they've left.

In the way a body remembers a touch,
long after it's been lost.

I will be the ache you cannot name.
The presence you cannot place.
The weight of something-
gone, but never really gone.

And if the world forgets me,
if history leaves me unwritten-
I will not beg to be kept.
I will not ask to be known.

Because it was never the world I wanted.
It was you.
Because even now-
I am at least near your breath.

19. What's left of love,

One word.
Five letters.

It means love.
It means kneeling at the altar of someone else's hands,
offering your ribs like they are nothing but loose change.

It means handing them the knife,
watching as they carve their name into your marrow,
scooping out the parts of you
that once felt untouched, untamed.

I opened my chest like an unlocked door,
let them walk in with mud on their boots,
let them rearrange the furniture of my heart
until I could no longer recognize the home I once was.

And when they left?
They didn't close the door.
Didn't look back at the wreckage.
Didn't wonder if the wind
would tear through the hollowed-out spaces
where I once kept my softness.

So I built walls.
Not brick, not stone-
something sharper.
A shell laced with barbed wire,
a lock that rusts before it turns.

Five letters.
One word.

I used to bleed it.
Now I won't even whisper it.

20. Blueprints of nothingness,

The human body is a masterpiece of failure.

Millions of red blood cells wage war to keep me
breathing,
thousands of nerves scream for me to feel,
oceans of water slosh inside me, dragging me forward-
and yet, beneath it all, there is a hollowness so vast,
it should have collapsed under its own gravity by now.

I am a sum of intricate systems,
perfect in function, disastrous in meaning.
I have a heart that pumps, but not one that knows why.
A body that moves, but no direction to give it purpose.
What is the point of being whole when you are empty?

I exist like a glitch in the universe's design,
a fraction of a fraction of something that never mattered.
A ghost still wrapped in its skin,
walking, talking, pretending it belongs here.

Casper would be proud-
I have reasoned my way into being nothing at all.

21. The thief and the verse.

She sat in the rust-bitten bus,
head against the rattling glass,
watching the city spit itself out in neon and smoke.

And there he was-poetry.
Not bound, not inked, not held by paper's frail arms,
but spilling through the cracks of existence,
a thing too untamed to be owned.

She caught glimpses of him in the rhythm of passing
headlights,
felt him settle under her skin,
pressing against the ribs like a truth too sharp to
swallow.

She didn't mean to read him,
but he wrote himself into her,
letter by letter, breath by breath,
until she carried him in the hollow between heartbeats.

She wanted to steal him-
fold him into the lining of her coat,
tuck him behind her teeth,
let him dissolve on her tongue like a forbidden psalm.

Not to keep. Not to cage.
Just to know, for a fleeting moment,
what it was like to taste eternity and call it her own

22. Drownin'

*Let's lock our eyes and throw the keys deep into the
ocean.
Let the salt strip us bare, let the tide gnaw at our bones.
Let the waves crush our ribs until we are nothing
but two bodies too stubborn to let go.*

*If you do not blink, neither will I.
If you do not move, neither will I.
If you hold your breath, I will drown beside you-
not in devotion, not in love,
but in the slow decay of what we swore would never
end.*

*But tell me, love,
when the water fills our lungs like a prayer we never
meant,
when our hands slip, when our names turn to salt on our
tongues,
when we are nothing but ghosts trapped beneath the
weight of our own making-
will you still call this love?*

*Or will you finally see-
we were never meant to float,*

only to sink beautifully?

And will you finally see-
that we were drowning long before the water ever
touched us?

23. Insignificance of Forever

What matters if nothing ends?
If the sky never caves, if the clock hands never twitch,
if love never flirts with the doorframe,
one foot in, one foot desperate to run—
what keeps it from rotting in its stillness?

Nothing.

Without an edge, there is no fear of falling.
Without a closing note, a song is just noise.
We would not write like our hands were on fire,
would not love like our ribs could crack from it,
would not scream just to hear the echo—
to know the world still spits us back.

If forever was promised,
we would beg for a thief to steal it.
We would slit the throat of eternity
just to hear it gasp.

24. Not a mosaic of everyone I've ever met.

I refuse to be stitched from the remnants of hands that have touched me,
a patchwork of borrowed glances, misplaced expectations,
a reflection twisted to fit the frame they hold me in.

I was not born to be rewritten,
not sculpted into familiarity for the comfort of those
who never bothered to know me.
I am not a canvas stretched to accommodate their colors,
not a verse edited until it forgets its own rhythm.

But if I strip away the layers they have pressed into my skin,
if I unlearn the names they have given me-
who is left?

Have I buried myself beneath their fingerprints?
Or was I never there at all?

Either way,
I will carve myself out of what remains,

even if it means setting fire to every version of me they built.

53

25. Filth in the marrow

There are days when I scrape my own skin just to feel
something,
when I sit in the bathtub and wonder -
if water could seep into my bones,
if drowning could start from the inside out.

Some pains are too precise to be washed away.
The world says stay clean,
but what do they know of filth
that stains from the marrow,
that clings even when you scrub?

A month goes by-thirty days of pretending.
I tell myself I am steel,
but I bend, crack,
splinter into the same old wounds.
It is muscle memory now-
the way grief makes a home out of my body,
how the walls of my mind cave in so easily.

And when the silence finally settles,
when the last tear falls into the stagnant water,
I am left with only one question-
is it really survival if it never stops hurting?

26. Temple in Ruin

*There is something humiliating about being seen like
this-
like sorrow worn too openly,
like a book left spine-up,
pages splayed for strangers to skim.*

*I do not need a hand on my shoulder,
a softened voice,
a look that lingers a second too long.
Pity is not kindness when it drips like condensation,
when it weighs heavier than the thing you're mourning
for me.*

*I have never asked to be saved,
never reached for someone else's version of solace.
I only ask to be left with my wreckage,
to sit with the ruin long enough
to make sense of what's left standing.*

*Because what if this is the only thing that feels real?
What if the breaking is the only thing that belongs to
me?
What if I do not wish to be held together,
but simply allowed to exist as I am-*

unfixed, unpolished, unsoftened?

And what if, just this once,
that could be enough?

27. Track Five

You don't remember the last time track five finished.

The one you called religion,
like it was a lifeline
drowning you in its repetition.
Survival had a soundtrack-
girls whispering into pillowcases,
boys who left your name unread,
and God-always silent,
playing deaf.

You swore you'd never forget.
Every lyric carved into your throat,
each verse a bullet you bit,
growing up meant bleeding without noise,
pretending the bridge didn't break you every time.
Reblogging poems like they were scripture,
calling collapse a rite of passage.

You loved songs like you loved people-
so loud, it became dissonance.
Now you flinch at the opening note
of the anthem that once saved your life.
You turn it down.

You skip.
You lie.

It's easier to pretend
you never needed that version of yourself-
the one with too much feeling,
too much mascara,
too much hope.
You outgrew her.
You abandoned her.
You betrayed her.

And maybe that's what growing up is-
not forgetting,
but listening and choosing silence anyway.

Or worse
hearing it in someone else's room,
and realizing the girl who bled to this song-
is now static between stations,
a ghost with your voice,
asking why you never came back.